# I'M TELLING ON YOU!

## Understanding and Dealing with Tattling

by
Richard L. Biren

illustrated by
Harry Norcross

A Tattling-Education Manual for Grades 2-5

# DEDICATION

To Cindy, my wife, friend, and colleague.

---

**OTHER BOOKS BY RICHARD L. BIREN PUBLISHED BY MAR✶CO PRODUCTS, INC.**

*I Wonder Who*
(A Friendship-Skills Program for Grades 4-8)

*Managing School Conflict*
(A Program to Decrease School Conflicts for Grades 4-8)

*Nah! Nah! Nah!*
(A Teasing-Education Manual for Grades 3-5)

*Don't Worry... Take Action*
(A Program for Handling Situations That Cause Worry for Grades 3-5)
Available Spring 2000

*I Can... I Will... I Did It!*
(A Program for Building Resiliency and Managing Change for Grades 3-5)
Available Fall 2000

**To Order, Call: 1-800-448-2197**

---

copyright © 1999
mar✶co products, inc.

Published by
mar✶co products, inc.
1443 Old York Road
Warminster, PA 18974
1-800-448-2197

All rights reserved including the right of reproduction in whole or in part in any form. The purchaser may reproduce the activity sheets, free and without special permission, for student use for a particular group or class. Reproduction of these materials for distribution to any person other than the purchaser or to an entire school system is forbidden.

Library of Congress Catalog Card Number: 99-64508
ISBN: 1-57543-075-4

Printed in the U.S.A.

# CONTENTS

## INTRODUCTION ... 4
- *I'M TELLING ON YOU* FORMAT ... 4
- USING *I'M TELLING ON YOU* ... 5
- TATTLING-LESSONS CHART ... 6

## TATTLING AWARENESS ... 7
- WHAT IS TATTLING? (GRADES 2-5) ... 8
  - HOME/SCHOOL TATTLING STUDENT EXAMPLES ... 10
  - HOME/SCHOOL TATTLING ... 11
- IS IT *TELLING* OR *TATTLING?* (GRADES 2-5) ... 12
  - TELLING OR TATTLING? ... 14
- WHY DO PEOPLE TATTLE? (GRADES 3-5) ... 15
  - WHY OTHERS TATTLE ... 17
  - WHY TATTLE? ... 18
- TATTLING AND FEELINGS (GRADES 2-5) ... 20
- REACTIONS TO TATTLING (GRADES 3-5) ... 22
  - REACTION CARDS ... 24

## DEALING WITH A TATTLER ... 25
- ASK THE TATTLER TO STOP (GRADES 2-5) ... 26
  - ASKING CHECKLIST ... 28
- USE AN "I" MESSAGE (GRADES 3-5) ... 29
  - "I" MESSAGES ... 31
- TALK WITH THE TATTLER (GRADES 4-5) ... 32
  - GUIDE TO TALKING WITH A TATTLER ... 34
- HOW DO I REACT? (GRADES 4-5) ... 35
  - HOW DO I REACT TO A TATTLER? ... 37
  - HOW COULD I REACT TO A TATTLER? ... 38
- HOW DO I TREAT THE TATTLER? (GRADES 2-5) ... 39
  - HOW DO I TREAT THE TATTLER? ... 41
- TREAT THE TATTLER WITH KINDNESS OR ATTENTION (GRADES 3-5) ... 42
- ASK OTHERS FOR HELP OR IDEAS (GRADES 3-5) ... 44
  - PLAN OF ACTION SAMPLE ... 46
  - PLAN OF ACTION ... 47
  - WHAT CAN I DO TO STOP THE TATTLING? ... 48

## MANAGEMENT TECHNIQUES ... 49
- TATTLER MANAGEMENT ... 50
  - SHOULD I TELL? ... 53
  - OTHER SUGGESTIONS ... 54

## BIBLIOGRAPHY ... 56

## ABOUT THE AUTHOR ... 56

# INTRODUCTION

Tattling most often occurs in the lower grades. As they grow and mature, most students stop tattling on others. Recognizing the unpleasant feelings, unkind actions, and resentment associated with tattling, they choose not to tattle.

For other students, tattling becomes a habit. It becomes an unhealthy way for them to deal with social difficulties. They rely on others to act for them. They fail to develop their own social abilities and skills.

This book is intended to help educators deal with tattling behavior. While tattling may reach its peak during the first two years of elementary school, it continues to be a problem for individual students beyond the early primary grades. To help educators deal with tattlers, this book presents lessons and suggestions the classroom teacher, school counselor, or social worker can use in a classroom setting or as part of a small-group counseling program.

## *I'm Telling On You* Format

This book is divided into three sections. The first section deals with tattling awareness. It consists of five lessons. These lessons help students realize what tattling is, what happens when tattling occurs, and why most students tattle.

The second section consists of seven lessons about dealing with a tattler. These lessons provide students with suggestions for dealing with someone who is tattling on them and gives them practice in implementing the suggestions.

The last section is for the educator using this book. It consists of suggestions about managing a tattler in the classroom. Using the suggestions will not only help to reduce or eliminate the tattling, but will also help create a more pleasant atmosphere for students to learn and grow and for the teacher to teach. The suggestions in the sections will also help the tattler accept more responsibility for his/her own behavior.

# Using *I'm Telling On You*

As an educator using this book, you will need to determine which lessons your students need. For example, a fifth-grade teacher may determine that all of her students already know the meaning of *tattling*. A mere review of the definition prior to presenting *Lesson 2 (Is It Telling or Tattling?)* would meet these students' needs.

On page 6, you will find a list of the lessons included in this book. Reproduce it and use it to check those lessons you wish to use. Write down the date the lessons are presented and comments about each one. This will help you keep track of specific lessons and evaluate their effectiveness.

Some lessons are more appropriate for older students and may need to be modified for use with younger students. The content of some lessons may be inappropriate for younger students. If some students in the group have poor reading skills, you may need to read the text on the worksheets to the entire group/class. Use your professional judgment about the students with whom you are working. Under each lesson on page 6, you will find suggested grade levels. These are only guidelines and should be regarded as such.

It's also important to remember that some students who tattle have other behavior problems. If you find tattling escalating beyond what you consider normal, the situation should be referred to others for additional assistance. The school counselor, social worker, school psychologist, or outside agencies such as social services or a mental health clinic may be able to offer assistance. Be aware of your limitations and remember that doing what's best for the student may mean referring him/her to someone with special expertise.

# TATTLING LESSONS

| LESSONS | USE | DATE/COMMENTS |
|---|---|---|
| **TATTLING AWARENESS:** | | |
| WHAT IS *TATTLING*? (GRADES 2-5) | | |
| IS IT *TELLING* OR *TATTLING*? (GRADES 2-5) | | |
| WHY DO PEOPLE TATTLE? (GRADES 3-5) | | |
| TATTLING AND FEELINGS (GRADES 2-5) | | |
| REACTIONS TO TATTLING (GRADES 3-5) | | |
| **DEALING WITH A TATTLER:** | | |
| ASK THE TATTLER TO STOP (GRADES 2-5) | | |
| USE AN "I" MESSAGE (GRADES 3-5) | | |
| TALK WITH THE TATTLER (GRADES 4-5) | | |
| HOW DO I REACT? (GRADES 4-5) | | |
| HOW DO I TREAT THE TATTLER? (GRADES 2-5) | | |
| TREAT THE TATTLER WITH KINDNESS OR ATTENTION (GRADES 3-5) | | |
| ASK OTHERS FOR HELP OR IDEAS (GRADES 3-5) | | |

# TATTLING AWARENESS

# WHAT IS TATTLING?
## (Grades 2-5)

**PURPOSE:** Students will learn the meaning of *tattling* and be able to give examples of tattling.

### MATERIALS NEEDED:

For each student: Copy of *Home/School Tattling* (page 11), pencil, crayons or markers
For the leader: *Home/School Tattling Student Examples* (page 10), overhead projector, screen, and transparency (optional); chalkboard and chalk or chart paper and marker

### PRE-LESSON PREPARATION:

Reproduce a copy of *Home/School Tattling* for each student.

Make a transparency of *Home/School Tattling Student Examples* (optional).

### LESSON:

**The leader should:**

Ask the students the following question:

*What is tattling?*

Allow the students to share their ideas about the meaning of the word *tattling*. When every student who wants to participate has had a chance to do so, state the following definition:

Tattling *is when you tell a person in authority (such as a parent, teacher, or other person in charge) that someone has made a mistake or has done something because you want to get that person in trouble with the authority.*

Ask the students to describe times when they remember someone tattling. Remind them not to use any names so those who were involved will not be unfairly identified. Allow enough time for the students to share their experiences. If none of the students provides examples of tattling, be prepared to give one or two examples of your own.

Distribute a copy of the *Home/School Tattling* activity sheet, a pencil, and crayons or markers to each student. Tell them to write about a tattling situation or draw a picture that represents tattling using word bubbles for what is being said. (For second- and third-grade students, you may wish to demonstrate the assignment by showing the students the transparency of *Home/School Tattling Student Examples* on an overhead projector.) Explain that each of the students should make one drawing or write about one situation that represents tattling at home and one that represents tattling at school. Tell the students that the situations described in their examples can be things that have actually happened or that they have imagined. Remind the students not to use any names. Tell the students how much time they have to complete this activity.

Ask each of the students to share one example from his/her paper. Remind them not to use any names or words that would put down anyone.

Write the following sentence stem on the chalkboard or chart paper:

    Tattling is _____ .

Direct the students to turn their papers over, copy the sentence stem from the chalkboard or chart paper, and complete it.

If time permits, ask the students to share their sentences with the group.

Conclude the lesson by repeating the definition of *tattling*.

# HOME/SCHOOL TATTLING STUDENT EXAMPLES

**2ND GRADE**

When you were gone, she used your comb on her hair.

**2ND GRADE**

Teacher, my partner keeps putting his hands on my desk.

**5TH GRADE**

She used your eyebrow pencil without asking.

**5TH GRADE**

Please tell the principal that someone in 5-D has cards at school.

Keep this a secret
OK
OK

# HOME/SCHOOL TATTLING

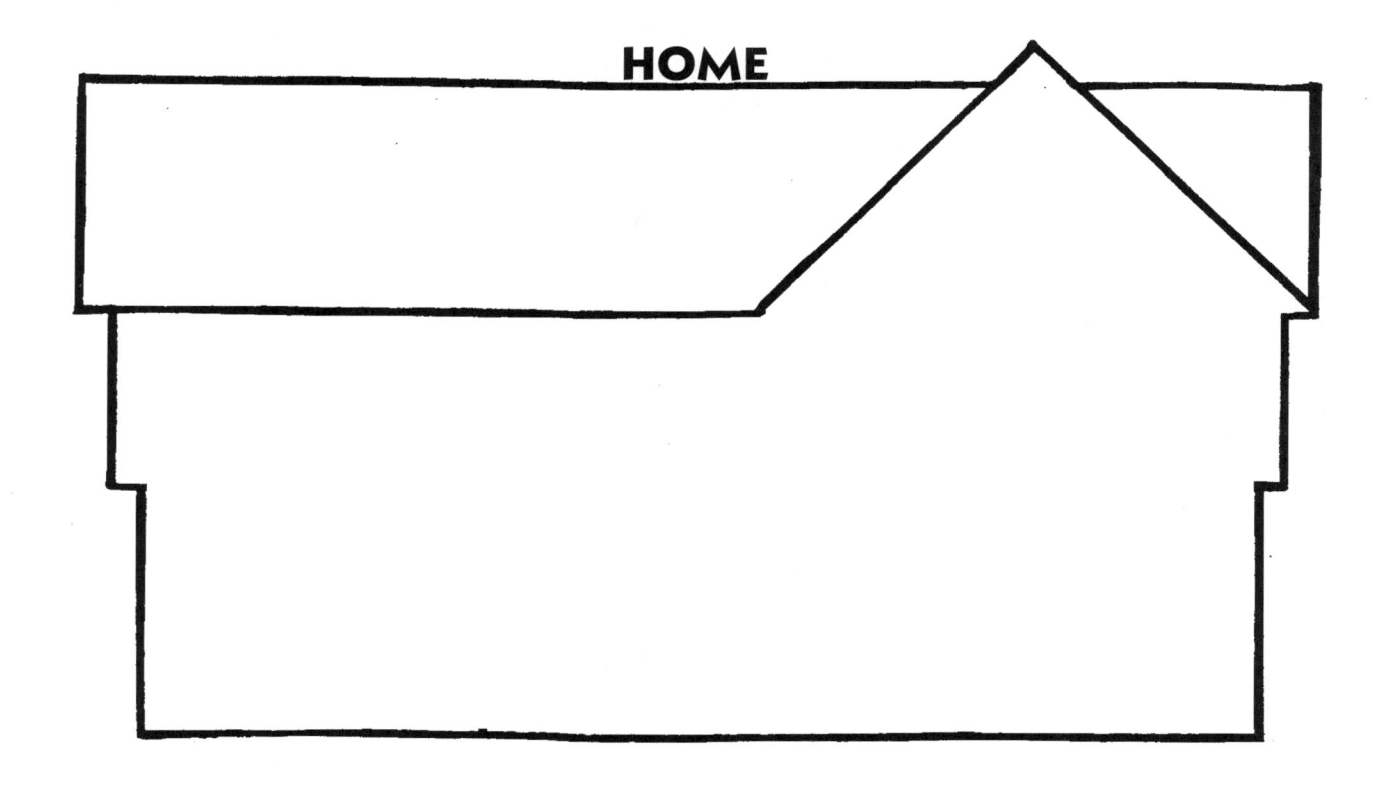

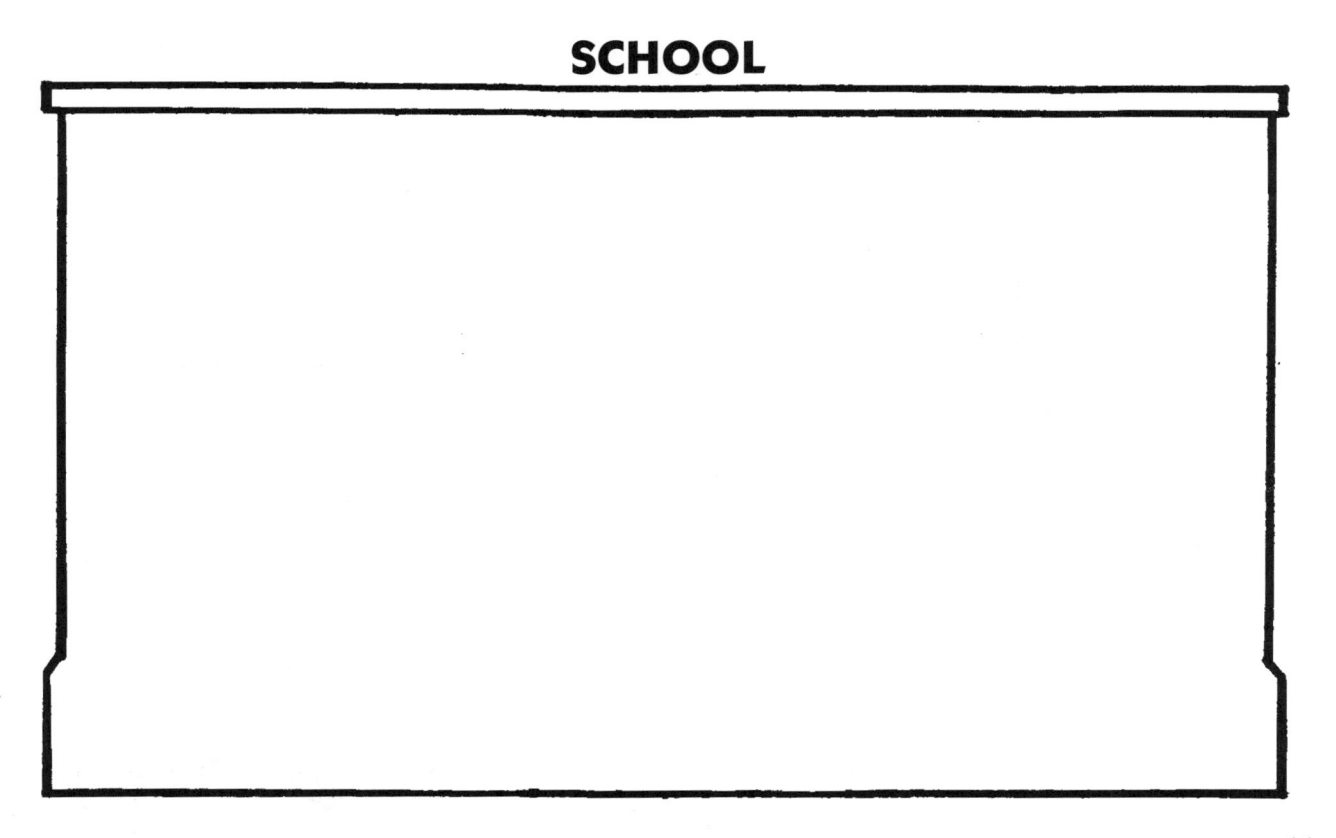

**HOME**

**SCHOOL**

# IS IT *TELLING* OR *TATTLING*?
## (Grades 2-5)

**PURPOSE:** Students will become aware of what tattling is and what it is not.

### MATERIALS NEEDED:

For each student: Copy of *Tattling or Telling?* (page 14), pencil
For the leader: None

### PRE-LESSON PREPARATION:

Reproduce a copy of *Tattling or Telling?* for each student.

### LESSON:

**The leader should:**

Ask the students the following question:

> *What is the difference between* tattling *and* telling?

Allow time for answers. Then share the following definitions with the group.

> Tattling *is telling a person in authority that someone has done something because you want to get that person into trouble with an authority.* Telling *is telling a person in authority that someone has done something because you want to obtain help for the person or the solve a problem.*

Ask the students to share examples of *telling* and *tattling*. Remind them not to use any names when sharing their examples. Correct any student misunderstandings and recognize good examples.

Distribute a copy of the *Tattling or Telling?* activity sheet and a pencil to each student. If you are working with older students, review the directions, answer any questions, and set a time limit for completion of the activity sheet. If you are working with younger students, read each item aloud and allow time for the students to respond.

When the students have finished, read each item on the activity sheet, starting with number 1. Have the students volunteer their answers. If any incorrect answers are given, ask the student to explain the reasoning behind his/her selection. Having the student do this enables the leader to better understand the student's thinking, and the student may even show that his/her viewpoint makes the answer correct. Recognize the students for their correct answers and correct any misunderstandings.

If time allows, ask the students to create examples of *telling* or *tattling* to share with the class. After everyone has had time to prepare, call on volunteers to share their examples with the group. Remind the students not to use any names and not to reveal whether their situation represents *tattling* or *telling*. After each volunteer has presented an example, ask the students to raise their hands and guess whether the example represents *tattling* or *telling*. Allow the volunteer to select which students will answer. When the correct answer is given, ask for another volunteer to present an example. Continue this process until every student who wishes to participate has had a turn or until the allotted time has elapsed. Recognize the students' correct answers and correct any misunderstandings.

Conclude the lesson by having the students explain the distinction between *tattling* and *telling*. Point to a student and say either "tattling" or "telling." The student will then give an example of whichever word was spoken. Do this with as many students as time will allow.

# TELLING OR TATTLING?

Directions: Check one box for each situation. Check *tell* for each situation that describes something that needs to be told to someone in authority. Check *tattle* for each situation that describes what appears to be tattling. Remember, if you're telling because someone needs help, it is *telling*. If you are telling to get someone in trouble for his/her behavior, it's *tattling*.

**1.** ☐ TELL ☐ TATTLE

"Jamal has gum in his pocket."

**2.** ☐ TELL ☐ TATTLE

"Kristen has a spot on her shirt."

**3.** ☐ TELL ☐ TATTLE

"Andrea is on the ground. She can't get up."

**4.** ☐ TELL ☐ TATTLE

"Flippe has a pencil. He's poking everyone who walks by his desk."

**5.** ☐ TELL ☐ TATTLE

"Mary isn't writing anything down."

**6.** ☐ TELL ☐ TATTLE

"Okano is crying. She won't tell me what's wrong."

**7.** ☐ TELL ☐ TATTLE

"Jasper is playing with his hair."

**8.** ☐ TELL ☐ TATTLE

"Mikey has the television on."

**9.** ☐ TELL ☐ TATTLE

"Juan is drawing pictures on his test paper."

**10.** ☐ TELL ☐ TATTLE

"Consuelo is taking my papers. I've asked her to stop, but she won't listen."

**11.** ☐ TELL ☐ TATTLE

"Gustavo is holding his leg, and tears are running down his face."

**12.** ☐ TELL ☐ TATTLE

"Michelle is daydreaming."

# WHY DO PEOPLE TATTLE?
## (Grades 3-5)

**PURPOSE:** To increase students' awareness of why others tattle and provide practice in identifying the reasons for tattling.

### MATERIALS NEEDED:

For each student: Copy of *Why Others Tattle* (page 17) and *Why Tattle?* (pages 18-19), pencil
For the leader: None

### PRE-LESSON PREPARATION:

Reproduce a copy of *Why Others Tattle* and *Why Tattle?* for each student.

### LESSON:

**The leader should:**

Ask the students the following question:

*Why do others tattle?*

Allow time for the students to answer.

Give each student a copy of the *Why Others Tattle* information sheet. Review the reasons with the group. Give examples, if needed, for each reason.

Distribute a copy of the *Why Tattle?* activity sheet and a pencil to each student. Review the directions with the group and set a time limit for completing the activity sheet. When the students have finished, read aloud each situation from *Why Tattle?* Call on the students to share their answers with the group. Recognize the correct answers and correct any misunderstandings.

If time allows, ask the students to create skits involving tattling. Divide the students into 2-4 member groups. Set aside a certain amount of time for the students to plan their skits. When the allotted time has elapsed, ask the groups to present their skits. As each skit is presented, ask the other students to look for possible reasons why the tattling occurs. When the skit is completed, have the students tell why they think the tattling occurred. When the students have finished guessing, have members of the group who performed the skit tell what *they* believe was the reason for the tattling.

Conclude the lesson by asking each student to give one reason why people tattle.

# WHY OTHERS TATTLE

1. **Fear of Consequences:** Some people are afraid that if they don't tattle, *they* will be punished or blamed for something that has happened or has been left undone. These people have probably been punished, some time in the past, for something that was the fault of someone else. By tattling, they hope to be held blameless.

2. **Rightness:** Some people tattle because they are determined to always have everything be right and in order. They base this feeling on how they view the world. These people are quick to point out the mistakes of others.

3. **Revenge:** Some people tattle to get even with someone who has hurt them in some way. They want the other person to hurt.

4. **Attention:** Some people tattle to get attention from others. When they tattle, they get someone to pay attention to their concerns and feelings.

5. **Security:** Some people tattle to make themselves appear to be better than others. They are quick to point out the mistakes of others.

6. **Control:** Some people tattle to make others do things. They get others to act against someone who is not acting properly. These tattlers get others to deal with *their* conflicts.

# WHY TATTLE?

Directions: As you read each situation, pretend that it has happened to you. Then write down the reason for tattling. You may refer to the *Why Others Tattle* information sheet to determine a reason.

1. Your younger brother spilled his cereal and milk on the kitchen floor. When your mom discovered it, she yelled at you and demanded to know why you hadn't told her immediately. She then sent you to your room. Now when your brother does something wrong, you tell your mom immediately.

   **Reason** _____

   _____

2. A student who sits next to you at school laughs whenever you give a wrong answer. One day, while looking at his worksheet, you notice a wrong answer. You approach the teacher and tell her about it. You think that will teach him to make fun of you.

   **Reason** _____

   _____

3. Your mom is always busy working outside the home during the day and busy with household duties in the evening. Even though he cleaned it up, you tell your mom that your brother spilled milk on the kitchen floor after school. Your mom puts her arms around you and thanks you for telling her. You enjoy it when she listens to you and hugs you.

   **Reason** _____

   _____

4. You don't get along with a classmate. Whenever you have a chance, you deliberately walk past her desk and stick your arm over her paper. When she moves your arm away, you run to the teacher to complain. The teacher looks at her and says, "Please keep your hands to yourself."

   **Reason** _____

   _____

5. The teacher has told everyone in class to use a pencil. You see a student using a pen. You approach your teacher and say, "Mrs. Patterson, Jamie's using a pen."

   **Reason** _____

   _____

6. A classmate, who is good in math, made a mistake on his paper. You are also good at math, and you want to have a higher grade than the other student. You tell the teacher about his mistake so you will get a better grade than he does.

   **Reason** _____

   _____

7. Several weeks ago, your older brother ran through the garden while everyone was playing hide-and-seek. When your dad discovered this, he grounded everyone for a week. He was upset because no one had told him about it. Last night, while playing again, your brother crushed the tulips in the garden. You quickly ran into the house and told your dad what had happened.

   **Reason** _____

   _____

# TATTLING AND FEELINGS
## (Grades 2-5)

**PURPOSE:** To increase students' awareness of how others feel when someone tattles on them.

### MATERIALS NEEDED:

For each student: Plain sheet of 8½" x 11" paper, crayons or markers, pencil
For the leader: Chalkboard and chalk or overhead projector, transparency, and marker

### PRE-LESSON PREPARATION:

None.

### LESSON:

**The leader should:**

Ask the students the following questions, pausing for responses before asking the next question.

*Would you please raise your hand if someone has ever tattled on you?*

*How did you feel when someone tattled on you?*

Say to the students:

*Today, I would like each of you to draw a picture of how you look when someone gets you into trouble by tattling. Draw a large face showing how you feel.* (On the chalkboard or transparency, draw an outline of the sheet of paper. Then, draw a tiny face in a corner of the page. The face you draw should be so small that the students will have difficulty seeing it.) *This is not how you should draw your face. You will have a whole sheet of paper. Use the whole sheet.* (Draw another outline on the paper, and this time draw a large oval for the face. Add the nose, eyes, mouth, hair, etc. Make everything large.) *This second picture is how big you need to draw your face. Use the whole paper. Draw a very large face.*

Distribute paper, a pencil, and crayons or markers to each student. Then remind the students by saying:

*Please draw a large face on your paper. The expression on the face should show how you feel when someone tattles on you. Remember to use the whole paper.*

As the students work, circulate around the room. Compliment those who have drawn large faces. Instruct those who haven't drawn large faces to erase their drawings or use the other side of the paper and try again. Check the students' drawings for appropriateness. Some students may draw smiling faces. If they do, ask if that is really how they feel when someone tattles on them. Allow the students time to draw and color their pictures.

Tell the students to put everything away except their papers. Then, tell the students that each of them will present his/her picture by walking to the front of the class/group and putting the paper in front of his/her own face. The other students will raise their hands if they can guess what feeling the paper face represents. When the correct feeling is guessed, another student will be given a turn. Continue until every student has presented his/her paper face.

Write the following sentence stem on the chalkboard/overhead projector:

Tattling makes others feel _____ .

Direct the students to turn their papers over, copy the sentence stem from the chalkboard/overhead projector, and complete it.

When everyone has finished, ask those students who wrote an unpleasant feeling to raise their hands. Briefly discuss the reasons for their answers and conclude that when someone is tattled on, he/she feels bad.

# REACTIONS TO TATTLING
## (Grades 3-5)

**PURPOSE:** To increase students' awareness of how others react to tattling and provide students with practice in showing how others react to tattling.

### MATERIALS NEEDED:

For each student group: Copy of *Reaction Cards* (page 24), scissors
For the leader: None

### PRE-LESSON PREPARATION:

Reproduce a set of *Reaction Cards* for each student group. Do not cut the cards apart.

### LESSON:

**The leader should:**

Ask the students the following questions. Pause for responses after each question and remind the students not to use any names when they share their answers.

*Would you please raise your hand if you have ever heard someone tattle?*

*What did the person who was tattled on do?*

*Would you please raise your hand if you think most people react to tattling with kind actions?*

*Would you please raise your hand if you think most people react to tattling with unkind actions?*

Divide the students into small 2-4 member groups. Have each group move to a desk or table where group members can work together. Distribute *Reaction Cards* and scissors to each group.

Read aloud the actions listed on the *Reaction Cards* sheet. Then, direct each group to cut its sheet into individual cards by cutting on the lines. If necessary, demonstrate how this should be done.

Tell the students to mix the cards together and place them, face down, on the desks/tables. Explain that they are going to practice different reactions to tattling. Each group member is to draw a card from the pile, read it aloud, and show the card to everyone in the group. Then, the student should pretend that someone has tattled on him/her, and role-play what it says on the card. Tell the group members that after the student has performed the reaction on the card, they are to give a "thumbs up" if they felt the action was performed correctly. (Note that the students do not give a "thumbs down" if the effort was not good.) Tell the students that they are not to give any "thumbs down" signals. Instead, if any group member thinks the action is incorrect, he/she should make a suggestion(s) for doing it correctly. The group should continue the activity until each member has had two turns.

Ask the students the following questions:

*How do most people react when someone tattles on them?* (The usual answer will be that most people react with an unpleasant action.)

*Do these actions make people feel good or bad?* (If desired, talk about each reaction and why each one could make the person feel bad.)

Conclude the lesson by stating that people react to tattling with unpleasant actions because being tattled on is an unpleasant experience.

| | |
|---|---|
| **SQUEEZE FACE AND STARE AT TATTLER**<br><br>I'M TELLING ON YOU: REACTION CARDS<br>© 1999 MAR✱CO PRODUCTS, INC. | **DENY:** *"NO, I DIDN'T DO IT."*<br><br>I'M TELLING ON YOU: REACTION CARDS<br>© 1999 MAR✱CO PRODUCTS, INC. |
| **YELL:** *"MIND YOUR OWN BUSINESS!"*<br><br>I'M TELLING ON YOU: REACTION CARDS<br>© 1999 MAR✱CO PRODUCTS, INC. | **BLAME:** *"THEY DID IT. I WAS JUST STANDING THERE."*<br><br>I'M TELLING ON YOU: REACTION CARDS<br>© 1999 MAR✱CO PRODUCTS, INC. |
| **THREATEN:** *"YOU JUST WAIT!"*<br><br>I'M TELLING ON YOU: REACTION CARDS<br>© 1999 MAR✱CO PRODUCTS, INC. | **TATTLE BACK:** *"SHE DID IT FIRST."*<br><br>I'M TELLING ON YOU: REACTION CARDS<br>© 1999 MAR✱CO PRODUCTS, INC. |
| **TEASE:** *"TATTLETALE! TATTLETALE!"*<br><br>I'M TELLING ON YOU: REACTION CARDS<br>© 1999 MAR✱CO PRODUCTS, INC. | **PLAY DUMB:** *"WHAT ARE YOU TALKING ABOUT?"*<br><br>I'M TELLING ON YOU: REACTION CARDS<br>© 1999 MAR✱CO PRODUCTS, INC. |
| **GIVE EXCUSE:** *"I COULDN'T SEE. SOMEONE PUSHED ME."*<br><br>I'M TELLING ON YOU: REACTION CARDS<br>© 1999 MAR✱CO PRODUCTS, INC. | **HIDE**<br><br>I'M TELLING ON YOU: REACTION CARDS<br>© 1999 MAR✱CO PRODUCTS, INC. |

# DEALING WITH A TATTLER

"I could use an 'I' Message."

"I could try discussing the problem."

"I could ask Laura to stop tattling."

# ASK THE TATTLER TO STOP
## (Grades 2-5)

**PURPOSE:** To increase students' awareness of how to ask someone to stop tattling and provide the students with practice in asking someone to stop tattling.

### MATERIALS NEEDED:

For each student: Copy of *Asking Checklist* (page 28), pencil
For the leader: Chalkboard and chalk or overhead projector, transparency, and marker

### PRE-LESSON PREPARATION:

Write the following steps on either the chalkboard or the overhead-projector transparency:

*Asking Steps:*

1. Look at the tattler. This is called *making eye contact.*
2. Use a pleasant, strong voice.
3. Ask the tattler to please stop what he/she is doing.
4. Thank the tattler for stopping.

### LESSON:

**The leader should:**

Tell the students:

> *One way to deal with someone who tattles on you is to ask him or her to stop. When making this request, you should do the following things.* (Read the *Asking Steps* written on the chalkboard or overhead transparency. After reading each step, demonstrate the incorrect way to do what it describes. Then demonstrate the correct way to do it.)

Select a volunteer to come in front of the group/class. Select someone who is likely to talk loudly enough for everyone to hear and who feels comfortable in front of the group. Using the *Asking Steps*, ask the volunteer to stop tattling on you.

*Example 1:*

Leader: Would you please stop tattling to the teacher every time I make a mistake?
Volunteer: Okay.
Leader: Thanks.

*Example 2:*

Leader: Would you please stop telling Mom when I use her makeup?
Volunteer: Why should I?
Leader: I would really appreciate it. (Smile) Thanks.

Direct the students to find partners.

Distribute a copy of the *Asking Checklist* and a pencil to each student. If you are working with younger students, read aloud the tattling situations and the directions on the *Asking Checklist*.

Tell the students to use the examples at the top of the page and take turns asking their partners to stop tattling. After each partner has role-played two situations, each student should complete the *Asking Checklist* for his/her partner. When all the students have finished, they are to give the checklist to their partners.

Conclude the lesson by saying:

*When someone tattles on you, follow the* Asking Steps *and ask the tattler to stop.*

# ASKING CHECKLIST

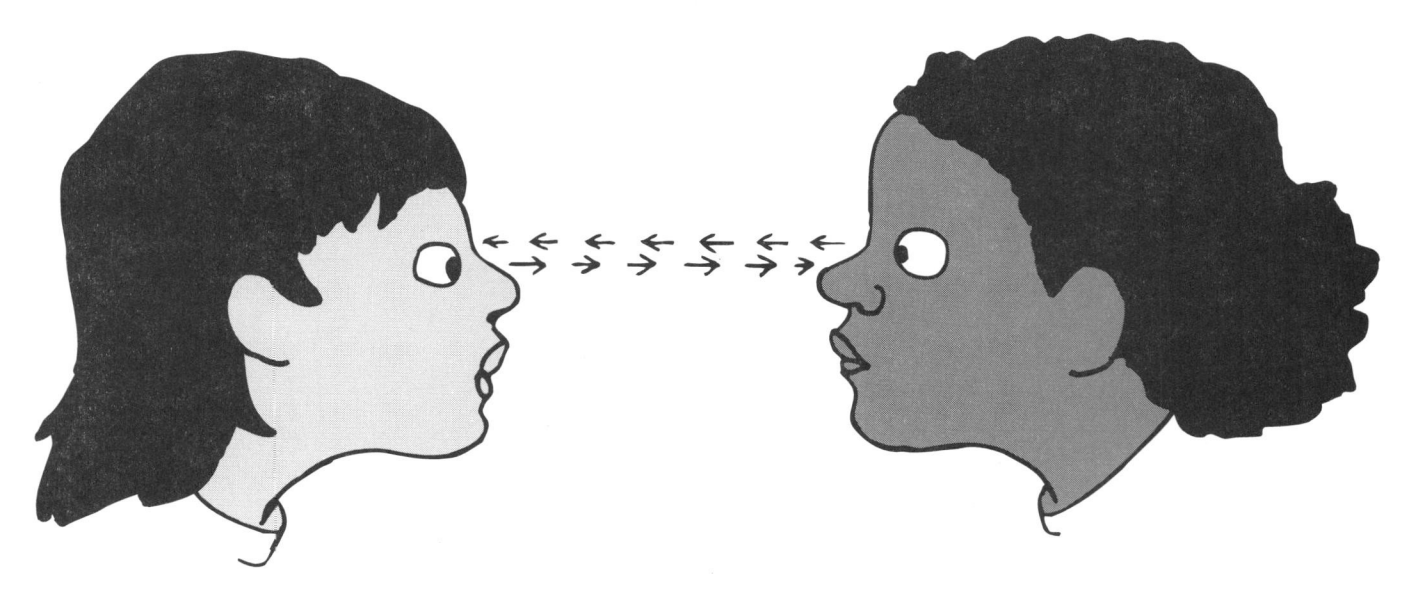

## Tattling Situations

1. Tattles whenever you don't use a pencil.
2. Tattles whenever you wear someone else's clothing.
3. Tattles whenever you don't do your chores on time.
4. Tattles whenever you touch something that belongs to someone else.

## *Asking* Steps

Directions: After your partner has asked you to stop tattling in two of the situations described above, check the items that describe what he/she did when asking.

☐ 1. Looked at me—made eye contact.

☐ 2. Used a pleasant, strong voice.

☐ 3. Asked me to please stop tattling.

☐ 4. Thanked me for not tattling any more.

# USE AN "I" MESSAGE
## (Grades 3-5)

**PURPOSE:** To provide students with an understanding of *"I" Messages* and practice in using them.

### MATERIALS NEEDED:

For each student: Copy of *"I" Messages* (page 31), pencil
For the leader: None

### PRE-LESSON PREPARATION:

Reproduce a copy of *"I" Messages* for each student.

### LESSON:

**The leader should:**

Tell the students:

> *Another way to talk with a tattler is to give an "I" Message. An "I" Message is when you tell the tattler how you feel and what actions caused you to feel the way you do. By using an "I" Message, you can let the tattler know how you feel. Sometimes tattlers are unaware of how their actions affect others. When you think the tattler is unaware of how you feel, try using an "I" Message.*

Distribute a copy of *"I" Messages* and a pencil to each student. Discuss the three parts of an *"I" Message* and what each part means. Then read and discuss the two examples. When everyone has finished reading and discussing examples, ask the students if there are any questions. Answer whatever questions the students have.

Tell the students to turn their papers over and write two *"I" Messages*. As they are writing, circulate among the students to check their progress.

Instruct the students to find a partner. Have the students say their *"I" Messages* to their partners. Set a time limit for this activity. When the activity is completed, have the students return to their regular seats.

Ask the students the following question. Allow enough time for responses.

*How did you feel when your partner gave you an "I" Message?*

Tell the students you are going to ask them a series of questions. If the answer to the question asked is "yes," the students are to raise their hands.

*Do you think an "I" Message would help a tattler understand how the other person feels?*

*Do you think knowing how tattling makes others feel would stop a tattler from tattling?*

*Would you use an "I" Message if someone tattled on you?*

Conclude the lesson by saying:

*When you think the tattler doesn't know how you feel, use an "I" Message.*

# "I" MESSAGES

## An *"I" Message* consists of three parts:

1. How you feel.

2. Action(s) that have made you feel this way.

3. What you would like to happen.

Example 1:

1. I feel upset
2. when you tattle on me.
3. Please stop.

Example 2:

1. I get angry
2. when you tell on me.
3. Would you please not do that again?

# TALK WITH THE TATTLER
## (Grades 4-5)

**PURPOSE:** To provide students with practice in talking to a tattler about solving a tattling concern.

### MATERIALS NEEDED:

For each student: Copy of *Guide to Talking With a Tattler* (page 34), pencil
For the leader: Chalkboard and chalk or overhead projector with transparency and marker (optional)

### PRE-LESSON PREPARATION:

Reproduce a copy of *Guide to Talking With a Tattler* for each student.

Prepare examples for each step on the *Guide to Talking With a Tattler* information sheet.

### LESSON:

**The leader should:**

Tell the students:

*One way to deal with a tattler is to talk with him or her. By discussing what's happening between the two of you, you can help each other better understand the situation and agree to do something about it.*

Distribute a copy of the *Guide to Talking With a Tattler* information sheet. Read the information on the guide with the group. Pause to give examples to clarify each step.

Ask for a volunteer to come before the group to pretend he/she has been tattling on you. With the volunteer, demonstrate the steps from the *Guide to Talking With a Tattler*. Allow time to answer any questions the students may ask.

Instruct the students to find a partner. Have the partners decide who will be the tattler and who will be the person being tattled on. Tell them that the person who is tattling tattles on a regular basis. Have the person being tattled on confront the tattler. The person being tattled on should follow the steps from the guide sheet and, through these, attempt to solve the tattling concern. Circulate around the room as the students are practicing to make sure they are following the steps correctly. Allow ample time for the students to complete this activity.

Have the students return to their regular seats. Ask them to turn the guide sheets over. Then tell them to write short answers for the following questions: (You may write the questions on a chalkboard or overhead-projector transparency.)

*How did you feel when your partner followed the steps on the guide sheet?*

*Do you feel that following the steps on the guide sheet would be helpful in solving a tattling concern?*

*Can you think of anything that would make the guide sheet work better?*

When the students have completed the activity, reread each question to the group and ask for volunteers to share their answers. Acknowledge good responses and correct any misunderstandings.

Conclude the lesson by saying:

*When someone is tattling on you, try talking to the person about what is happening.*

# GUIDE TO TALKING WITH A TATTLER

1. Choose a time when you can meet with the tattler without others around to distract you.

2. Choose a time when the tattler is likely to be in a good mood.

3. Start by asking the tattler if there was something you did that caused him/her to tattle on you. Use questions like:

   *Are you mad at me?*
   *Did I do something that made you want to tattle on me?*
   *Are you upset with me because of something I've done?*

4. If a tattler tells you that something you do makes him/her tattle, discuss how you can deal with that behavior so he/she won't tattle.

5. If the tattler doesn't answer your questions, ask him/her to think about what can be done to stop the tattling. Use questions like:

   *What would you like me to do?*
   *Is there anything you can do to stop tattling on me?*
   *Is there anything I can do to help you stop tattling on me?*

6. If a tattler tells you what might help stop the tattling, plan actions you both will do and thank the tattler for his/her help.

7. If the tattler hasn't answered any of your questions, describe what you would like to see happen. Try to make a suggestion(s) that will help each of you.

8. If the tattler agrees with your suggestion(s), plan actions you each will take and thank the tattler for his/her help.

9. If the tattler doesn't wish to do anything about the situation, thank him/her for listening and walk away.

# HOW DO I REACT?
## (Grades 4-5)

**PURPOSE:** To increase the students' awareness of their reactions when tattled on and provide other alternatives for them to use.

## MATERIALS NEEDED:

For each student: Copy of *How Do I React to a Tattler?* (page 37) and *How Could I React to a Tattler?* (page 38), pencil
For the leader: Chalkboard and chalk or overhead projector with transparency and marker

## PRE-LESSON PREPARATION:

Reproduce a copy of *How Do I React to a Tattler?* and *How Could I React to a Tattler?* for each student.

## LESSON:

**The leader should:**

Tell the students that in this lesson, they will be learning about how people react when they are tattled on. Tell them to think about what they have seen happen when someone is tattled on. Then ask the students the following questions. Allow time for answers. Write, or have a student write, the students' responses on the overhead transparency or on the chalkboard.

> *What are some of the ways a person looks when someone is tattling on him or her?*
>
> *What are some of the things people say?*
>
> *What are some of the gestures people use?*

Then ask these questions:

> *Do you think these reactions give the tattler control?* (In most cases, the answer will be *yes*.)

*Does the tattler know that he or she can get the other person to react in a certain way by tattling on him or her?* (If the tattling is frequent and the person being tattled on reacts in a certain way each time, then the answer is *yes*.)

*Do you think a tattler might tattle in order to gain control?* (Yes.)

Read the following example to the students:

*A younger brother frequently tattles on his older sister. When the older sister hears about it, she raises her clenched fist toward her brother. She shakes it and yells, "I'm going to get you!" When she does this, the brother immediately tells Mom, who confronts the sister and sends her to her room. Because the little brother knew his sister was likely to react by shaking her fist, he was able to control her. He had her sent to her room with the help of Mom. Raise your hand if you think a tattler might tattle in order to gain control.*

Tell the students they are going to examine how they react when someone tattles on them. Distribute a copy of *How Do I React to a Tattler?* and a pencil to each student. Read the directions with the students and answer any questions. Then, depending on the age of the students, either have them read the items on the activity sheet or read the items to them. Allow enough time for the students to complete the activity sheet.

Ask the following questions when the activity sheet has been completed. Allow enough time for the students to respond. Write the answers, if you wish, on the chalkboard or on the overhead-projector transparency.

*Would you please raise your hand if you react in ways that allow a tattler to control you?*

*How could you react so a tattler won't be encouraged to tattle on you?*

Distribute a copy of *How Could I React to a Tattler?* to each student. Read the directions with the students and answer any questions. Direct the students to complete items 1-8 on the activity sheet. Allow enough time for them to complete all the items.

When everyone has finished, have the students complete the sentence stem at the bottom of the page.

The next time someone tattles on me, I will _____ .

Conclude the lesson by saying:

*When someone tattles on you, try acting positively toward him or her.*

# HOW DO I REACT TO A TATTLER?

Directions: For each of the items below, place a check in the box next to each reaction you have had after someone has tattled on you. For numbers 8 and 9, write in other reactions you have had.

1. ☐ Yelled/Screamed/Shouted

2. ☐ Threatened the tattler with gestures (such as shaking a closed fist)

3. ☐ Threatened the tattler with words (such as, "Just you wait!")

4. ☐ Frowned

5. ☐ Stared at the tattler, showing a mad face

6. ☐ Turned red in the face from embarrassment

7. ☐ Snuck away to hide

8. ☐ _____

9. ☐ _____

# HOW COULD I REACT TO A TATTLER?

Directions: For each of the items below, check those actions you could do if someone tattled on you. For number 8, write another positive reaction you could take.

1. ☐ Think about something pleasant

2. ☐ Stay calm

3. ☐ Keep my hands by my side

4. ☐ Smile

5. ☐ Admit what I have done

6. ☐ Use a pleasant voice

7. ☐ Use caring language

8. ☐ _____

The next time someone tattles on me, I will _____
_____
_____ .

38

# HOW DO I TREAT THE TATTLER?
## (Grades 2-5)

**PURPOSE:** To increase the students' awareness of the negative things they do to a tattler and help them become aware of actions they could take to stop the tattler.

### MATERIALS NEEDED:

For each student: Copy of *How Do I Treat the Tattler?* (page 41), pencil
For the leader: None

### PRE-LESSON PREPARATION:

Reproduce a copy of *How Do I Treat the Tattler?* for each student.

### LESSON:

**The leader should:**

Tell the students:

> *Sometimes others tattle because they've been treated badly. They attempt to get even. They think, "You make my life miserable, so I'll make your life miserable." They seek revenge for the pain they have felt. They do not realize that by tattling, they create difficulties.*

> *Whenever you suspect someone is tattling to get even, it's good to examine your own actions. If you haven't been nice, changing your behavior might eliminate the tattling problem. Stopping unkind actions can stop tattling.*

Distribute a copy of *How Do I Treat the Tattler?* and a pencil to each student. Tell the students:

> *On your sheet, is a list of common behaviors that people use when someone tattles on them. Look at each one.* (Note: If the students cannot read, tell them you will read each item aloud.) *Respond by thinking of the times someone tattled on you. How did you treat the tattler? When you think of tattlers, remember to consider not only classmates, but also family members, such as brothers and sisters, neighbors, and friends.*

Answer any questions the students might have and then direct them to complete the activity sheet. Allow enough time for them to complete the activity sheet.

Tell the students to look at those items they have checked. Then, divide the students into 2-4 member groups. Instruct each group to create a skit in which a tattler is mistreated. Then, each group should prepare a second skit in which the tattler is treated nicely. Allow time for the students to create and practice their skits. (Note: If the students need further clarification, ask for volunteers to role-play a skit in front of the group. Then, provide ideas or suggestions about what the groups might do in a skit.)

Have each small group present its skit. Recognize good efforts and correct any misunderstandings. After each group has performed its skit, ask the students:

*If you were a tattler, how would you feel if someone treated you nicely like this?*

*Would you stop tattling on a person who was nice to you?*

Conclude the lesson by saying:

*Whenever someone is regularly tattling on you, think about any unkind things you may do to the tattler. Stop being unkind and try treating the tattler nicely.*

# HOW DO I TREAT THE TATTLER?

Directions: Place a check in the box next to each thing you do.

1. ☐ I ignore the tattler.

2. ☐ I tease the tattler in a hurtful manner.

3. ☐ I put the tattler down with my comments.

4. ☐ I avoid looking at the tattler.

5. ☐ I don't include the tattler in games I play.

6. ☐ I call the tattler unkind names.

7. ☐ I hit or push the tattler.

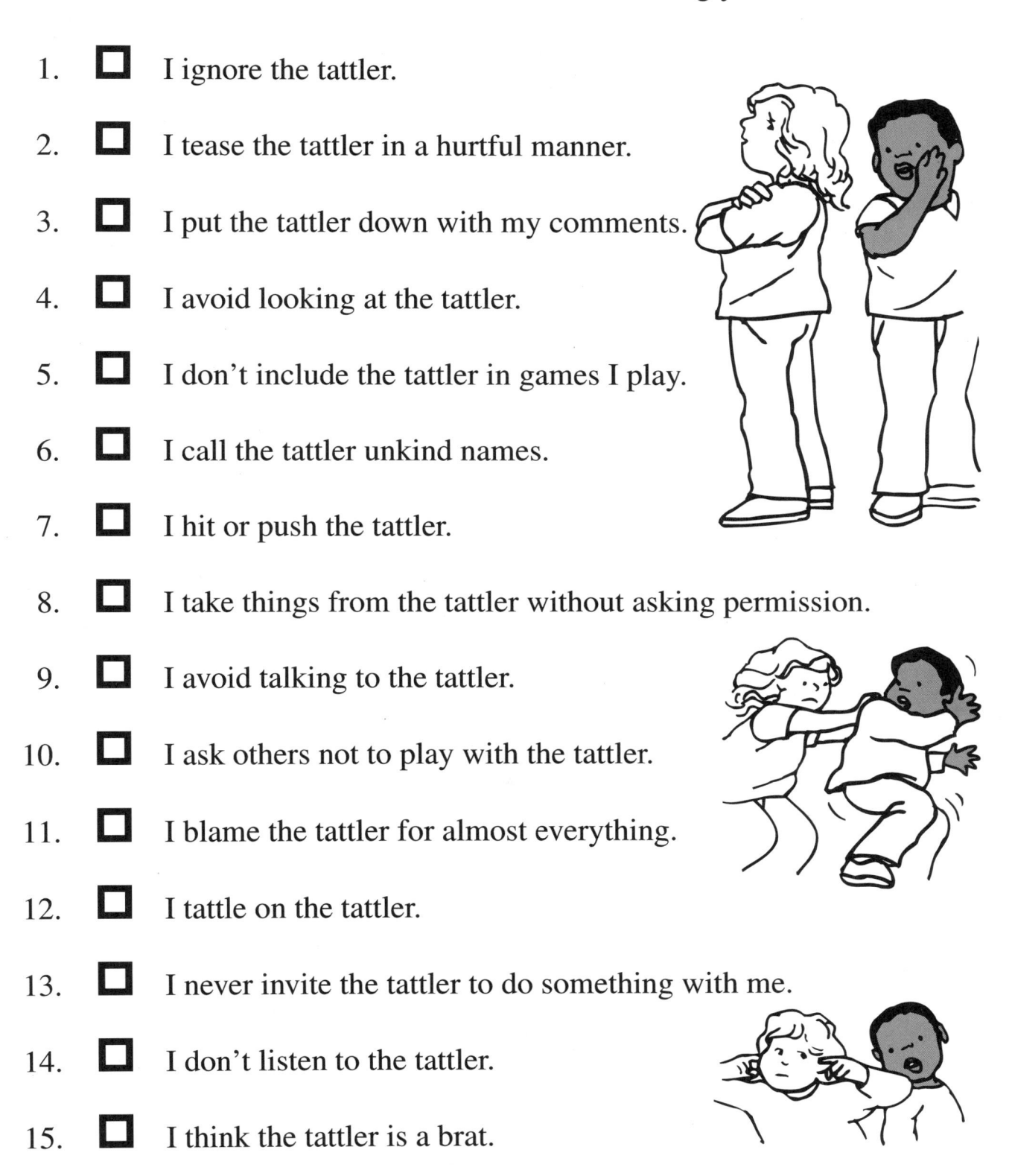

8. ☐ I take things from the tattler without asking permission.

9. ☐ I avoid talking to the tattler.

10. ☐ I ask others not to play with the tattler.

11. ☐ I blame the tattler for almost everything.

12. ☐ I tattle on the tattler.

13. ☐ I never invite the tattler to do something with me.

14. ☐ I don't listen to the tattler.

15. ☐ I think the tattler is a brat.

# TREAT THE TATTLER WITH KINDNESS OR ATTENTION
## (Grades 3-5)

**PURPOSE:** To provide the students with suggestions for and practice in giving positive attention to a tattler.

## MATERIALS NEEDED:

For each student group: Sheet of paper, pencil
For the leader: Overhead projector, transparency, and marker or chalkboard and chalk

## PRE-LESSON PREPARATION:

Write the following questions on the chalkboard or overhead transparency:

   What compliments could you give to a tattler?
   What could you share with a tattler?
   What activities could you do with a tattler?

## LESSON:

**The leader should:**

Tell the students:

> *Some people tattle in order to gain attention. If you give these people attention in positive ways, it may reduce or even eliminate the tattling. Some tattlers who receive negative comments for their tattling will continue to tattle in order to get attention because they receive very little attention elsewhere.*

> *If you suspect someone is regularly tattling on you to get attention, try giving the tattler attention in other ways. Complimenting, sharing, or doing something with the tattler may help stop the tattling.*

Divide the students into 2-4 member groups. Distribute paper and pencil to each group. Direct each group to select a secretary to write responses on the paper. Tell the students that each group needs to select one of the questions written on the chalkboard/overhead projector and create a list of possible answers to it. Answer any questions the students have and tell them how much time they have to complete the activity. As the students are working, circulate among the groups, checking their progress and encouraging their efforts.

Ask the group secretaries to read their group's question and list of possible actions to the entire class. Recognize good work and correct any misunderstandings.

Direct each student to find a partner and prepare a skit to be presented in front of the entire class. The skit should demonstrate how the partners might carry out one of the actions mentioned in the lists. Tell the students how much time they have to prepare their skits.

Have the partnerships present their skits to the entire group. After each skit has been presented, thank the partners for their effort.

Conclude the lesson by saying:

*When someone is tattling on you in order to get attention, give the tattler attention by complimenting, sharing, or doing something nice with him or her.*

# ASK OTHERS FOR HELP OR IDEAS
## (Grades 3-5)

**PURPOSE:** To increase the students' awareness of resources that may help them deal with a tattler and provide practice in using a plan of action to solve a tattling problem.

### MATERIALS NEEDED:

For each student: Copy of *Plan of Action Sample* (page 46), *Plan of Action* (page 47), and *What Can I Do to Stop the Tattling?* (page 48); pencil
For the leader: Chalkboard and chalk or overhead projector with transparency and marker

### PRE-LESSON PREPARATION:

Reproduce a copy of *Plan of Action Sample, Plan of Action,* and *What Can I Do to Stop the Tattling?* for each student.

### LESSON:

**The leader should:**

Tell the students:

> *When someone continues to tattle after you have tried different ways to get him or her to stop, you may need to ask someone else for assistance. Parents, teachers, counselors, and others you know may be able to offer suggestions that would help. If a teacher or parent is involved in the actual tattling, talking to him or her about the situation can help. Making the tattler aware of what's happening and how you feel about it, will help him or her to understand your situation. Working with a parent or teacher, you can plan actions one or both of you can take to stop the tattling.*

Distribute a copy of *Plan of Action Sample, Plan of Action,* and *What Can I Do to Stop the Tattling?* and a pencil to each student. Discuss the four parts of the *Plan of Action Sample* and review the example. To make the concept more clear, ask a student to describe a specific tattling problem. Remind the students not to use any names. Using the chalkboard or overhead transparency, complete an action plan for this problem by writing down suggestions from the students for each part. Emphasize that not everyone will agree with the plan and that that's okay. Only the people writing a plan need to agree with it. What works for one situation and person may not work for others.

Have the students form partnerships. Tell them to pretend that one partner is a parent or teacher and the other is a student with a tattling problem. The partners are to discuss the tattling problem and together complete a *Plan of Action* to solve it. They may use *What Can I Do to Stop the Tattling?* as a reference. Remind the students not to use any names in the plan. Allow plenty of time for the students to complete this activity.

Ask for volunteers to share their completed plan with the entire group. Thank those who share their plans and recognize their good work. Correct any misunderstandings.

Tell the students:

> *Raise your hand if you think discussing tattling with a teacher or parent and completing a plan of action would help to solve the problem.*

Conclude the lesson by saying:

> *When someone continues to tattle after you have taken different actions, ask others for help and suggestions.*

# PLAN OF ACTION SAMPLE

## A basic *Plan of Action* consists of the following parts:

1. Statement of the problem

2. Action(s) to solve the problem

3. Time and/or date when the action(s) will be performed

4. Result of the action(s)

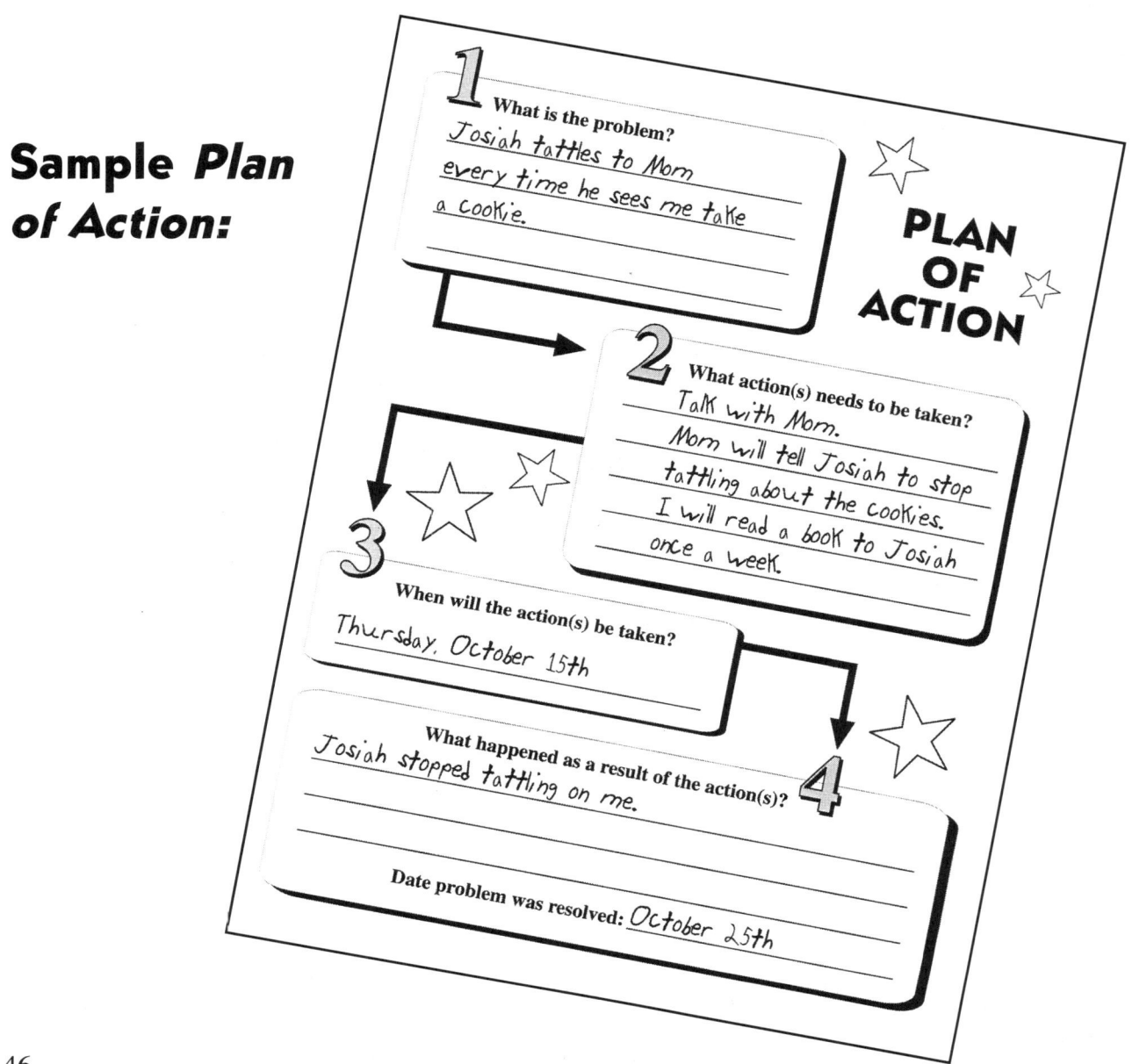

**Sample *Plan of Action*:**

**PLAN OF ACTION**

**1. What is the problem?**
Josiah tattles to Mom every time he sees me take a cookie.

**2. What action(s) needs to be taken?**
Talk with Mom. Mom will tell Josiah to stop tattling about the cookies. I will read a book to Josiah once a week.

**3. When will the action(s) be taken?**
Thursday, October 15th

**4. What happened as a result of the action(s)?**
Josiah stopped tattling on me.

Date problem was resolved: October 25th

# PLAN OF ACTION

**1. What is the problem?**
_____
_____
_____

**2. What action(s) needs to be taken?**
_____
_____
_____
_____

**3. When will the action(s) be taken?**
_____

**4. What happened as a result of the action(s)?**
_____
_____
_____

Date problem was resolved: _____

# WHAT CAN I DO TO STOP THE TATTLING?

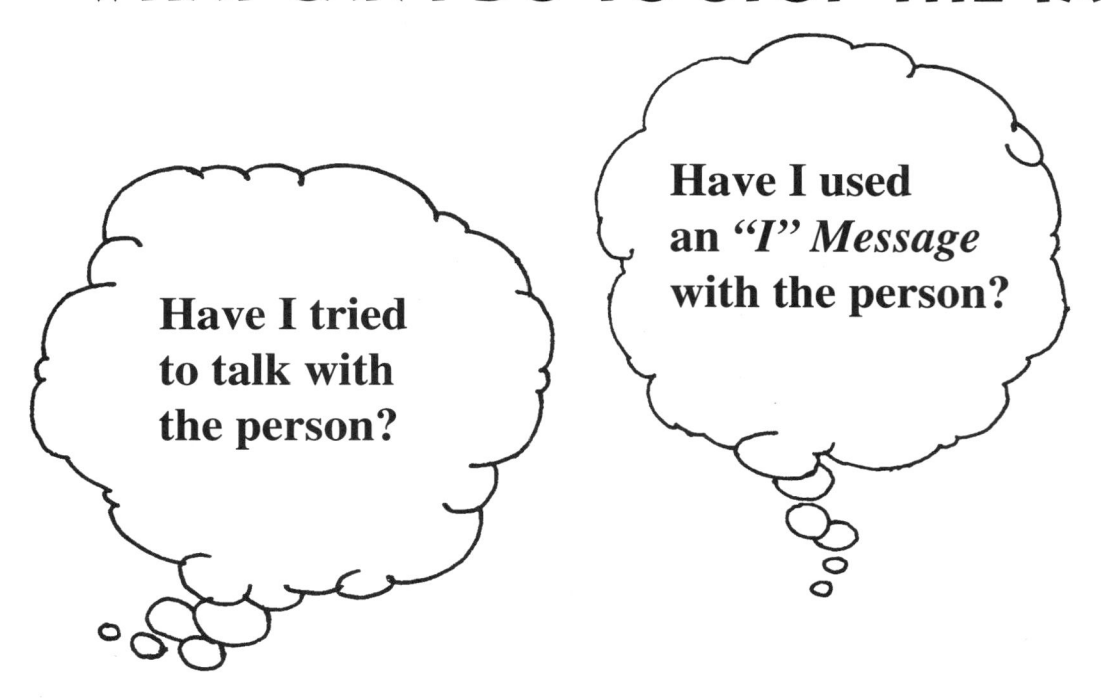

Have I tried to talk with the person?

Have I used an *"I" Message* with the person?

Have I asked the person to change how he/she acts?

Have I been unkind to the person?

Do I need to stop my unkind actions?

Have I reacted to tattling by allowing the person to control me?

How can I change my reactions to tattling?

Have I treated the person with kindness?

Have I completed a *Plan of Action?*

Have I asked others to help me deal with the situation?

# MANAGEMENT TECHNIQUES

# TATTLER MANAGEMENT

Managing a tattler can be difficult. Most tattlers who tattle in school have had practice at home and their behavior has reached the habit stage by the time they reach school age. Habits are sometimes hard to break. However, with guidance from a teacher, counselor, or parent, this habit can be broken.

As educators, most of us have experienced times when the tattler wants us to do something about the situation he/she reports. For example, I recall a first-grader who came close to setting the world's record for tattling in a five-minute period.

I was presenting a weekly guidance lesson. After I finished giving the class the week's assignment, a boy approached me. He told me that another student was not using a pencil. I thanked him and reminded the offending student to use a pencil for her drawing. Within 30 seconds, the same boy approached me again. This time, he was complaining that a different student had hit him as he went to the pencil sharpener. This time, I reminded the students to keep their hands and feet to themselves. Within the next minute, the same boy complained that someone was thinking about putting things on his desk. I told him not to worry about it. A minute later, the same boy got up to get a drink. As he walked past a particular student's desk, he slowed and leaned over the student who was sitting down. The seated student immediately waved his hand and said, "Get away!" Guess who tattled again?

With all his tattling, you can imagine that I was becoming a little irritated, especially when the tattler deliberately provoked the last situation. I needed to do something to get him to stop. I decided the tattler needed to change his actions. I told him that if he needed to get up, he was to walk outside all of the desks in the room and to stay at least five feet away from the other students' desks. With that directive, he stopped tattling.

As I later analyzed what had happened, I realized that I encouraged the boy to tattle by acting on his concerns. It was as if this tattler was "pulling my strings" to get at the other students with whom he had problems. Once I forced the tattler to change his actions, the tattling stopped.

I relate this example because I believe tattling becomes annoying for many of us when we have somehow acted in a way that encourages the tattler to continue. If we allow the tattler to draw us into the act, he/she often will continue doing it. On the other hand, if we can direct the tattler to focus on what he/she can do about the problem, we can change the tattler's behavior.

Let me relate another example.

> One day, I was working cafeteria duty. A girl raised her hand and complained about a student making faces. This student was sitting about 20 feet away from the tattler. For her to see the faces, she would have to have strained her neck muscles.
>
> I informed the tattler not to look at the student making the faces. I also assured her that I would watch the area. Within two minutes, this same student raised her hand again and complained about the same thing. Since the tattler had not done what I suggested, I immediately moved *her* to another part of the cafeteria. She was upset that I hadn't done anything to the person who was supposedly making the faces. I told her this new seat should prevent the face maker from bothering her again. She had expected me to act against the other student. She had expected me to act *for her.*
>
> Two days later, this same girl complained about someone making unkind remarks about her. All the students claimed they were talking nicely. Within two minutes, this girl complained again. I moved her and the student she complained about to separate areas of the cafeteria. The tattler was once again upset with me. I assured her that the unkind remarks should stop and, if they didn't, she should let me know. She had tattled because she wanted me to act in a particular way. She wanted me to do something to the person who supposedly was unkind to her. When I

forced her to move, which in essence *was* doing something about it, she became upset. However, forcing the tattler to be involved in the solution solved the problem. She never tattled to me again.

As you deal with tattlers, be careful to examine what *you* do. Ask yourself:

Do I encourage the tattler?

Do my actions give the tattler what he/she wants?

Do my actions make it possible for the tattler to do nothing?

Is the tattler forcing me to act for him/her?

In addition to examining your own actions, it's important to direct the tattler to focus on what he/she is doing. The following questions may be helpful for a student to review before tattling.

If I tell, will I:

help someone?

prevent someone from being hurt?

prevent something from being broken or damaged?

If the student can answer *yes* to any of these questions and can say that he/she has done all he/she can to help resolve the situation, then it's okay to tell someone about it. When working with a tattler, reproduce *Should I Tell?* (page 53) to use as a reference.

# SHOULD I TELL?

**If I tell, will I:**

help someone?

keep someone from being hurt?

keep something from being broken or damaged?

**If you have done all you can to solve the problem and you can answer *yes* to any of the questions above, then you should tell a parent, teacher, counselor, or other adult what has happened.**

# OTHER SUGGESTIONS

Additional suggestions include:

1. **Discuss the differences between *tattling* and *telling*.** If a student is tattling regularly, it's important to discuss the behavior with him/her. Knowing the difference between *telling* what should be told and *tattling* is essential for the student's improvement. Make sure the student understands the differences and how to determine what needs to be told and what doesn't. Clarifying this is sometimes all that is needed for the student to discontinue the tattling.

2. **Know what is happening.** If you're not sure what might be happening, keep a list of when the tattling occurs, who's involved, what's tattled about, and your reactions. Over the course of a week or two, a pattern may develop. The tattling may involve certain people. If it's always the same person, this may indicate that a conflict exists. Ask the tattler what that person does that bothers him/her. If necessary, schedule a meeting to discuss the situation with all concerned. Plan a solution that will help everyone. Solving the "real" problem may stop the tattling.

3. **Move the tattler to a new location.** If the tattling is directed at others who sit nearby, perhaps a move to a different location would help. This may involve isolating the tattler from the rest of the students. Sometimes a tattler needs to realize that he/she cannot be with others if he/she is going to annoy them. The move should be discussed with the tattler, letting him/her know that if the tattling stops, he/she will be allowed to return to sitting with the others or to a location of his/her choice. This provides motivation for the tattler to change. It also relieves everyone of the annoyance of tattling.

4. **Keep track of the tattling.** The tattler may sometimes be unaware of how often the tattling is actually taking place. Discuss the tattling situation with the tattler. Then, tape a 3" x 5" index card to the top of the tattler's desk. Do not label the card *tattling*. This helps keep the student from being unnecessarily embarrassed. Every time he/she tattles, the card is marked with a check. Check the card at the end of the day or week. Discuss the number of checks and ways the tattler might reduce or eliminate the tattling. Encourage the tattler to change. Continue to keep track of his/her tattling on an index card and check the tattler's progress. Set target numbers to reach and recognize improvement.

5. **Have the tattler make positive statements.** Another way to stop tattling and bring about changed behavior is to require the tattler to state at least two positive things about a person before he/she is allowed to tattle on him/her. This forces the tattler to look for good and not focus only on negative behavior. Another advantage of this method is that the amount of effort required to tattle has dramatically increased. Some tattlers decide the price is too great and soon stop.

6. **Determine whether the tattler is seeking attention.** Determine if tattling is being used as a way for the student to get attention from other students. Even though this attention is likely to be negative for the tattler, it's better than no attention at all. If you find that the student has difficulty interacting with others, arrange for the student to receive help to develop his/her social skills. Presenting lessons to the entire class, counseling the student individually, and/or placing the child in a social-skills group would help develop social skills. Using these skills could lead to positive attention from peers and reduce or eliminate tattling.

# BIBLIOGRAPHY

Albert, Linda. *A Teacher's Guide to Cooperative Discipline.* Circle Pines, MN: American Guidance Services, 1989.

Bozzone, Meg A. "Spending Less Time Refereeing and More Time Teaching." *Instructor:* July/August 1994, pp. 88-91.

Collins, Dwane R. and Myrtle T. Collins. *Survival Kit for Teachers (and Parents).* Santa Monica, CA: Goodyear, 1975.

Crary, Elizabeth. *Kids Can Cooperate.* Seattle, WA: Parenting Press, 1984.

DeBruyn, Robert L. and Jack L. Larson. *You Can Handle Them All.* Manhattan, KS: The Master Teacher, 1984.

Erickson, Dr. Martha. "Tattles." *Growing Concerns Column,* http://www.cyfc.umn.edu/children/concerns/tattle.html. April 23, 1996.

Schaefer, Charles E. and Howard L. Millman. *How to Help Children with Common Problems.* St. Louis, MO: Mosby, 1981.

# ABOUT THE AUTHOR

Richard L. Biren is a licensed elementary-school counselor in Brush, Colorado with more than 20 years experience working with students at the elementary level. He also has five years experience as a school counselor at the junior high/high school level in Minnesota and North Dakota and has taught at the community-college level.

He holds BS and MS degrees from North Dakota State University and an Elementary Counselor Endorsement from Colorado State University. For the past 11 years, he has reviewed books as a professional library advisor for the National Education Association.

In addition to teaching and counseling, Richard has written successful grant proposals for career education and bibliotherapy. He has also published articles in regional counseling journals and newsletters.

Richard lives in Brush with his wife, Cindy, and their two children, Becca and Jim.